LORD
of time

by FRANK TOPPING

Illustrations by Carol MacMahon

LUTTERWORTH PRESS
Cambridge

Topping, Frank
  Lord of time
  1. Devotional literature
  I. Title
  242   BV 4832.2

  ISBN 0 7188 2618 3

First published in 1985 by
Lutterworth Press, 7 All Saints' Passage, Cambridge CB2 3LS

By the same author: *Lord of the morning*
                    Lord of the evening
                    Lord of my days
                    Lord of life
                    Working at prayer
                    The Words of Christ

Additional illustration on p. 29 by Morris Walker

Printed in Great Britain

To A S Berry

with gratitude for adventures shared
from the Solent to the Sea of Galilee

CONTENTS

TIME TO LIVE

Lord,
I would like my life
to be full.
I would like
to learn things,
to have a keen interest
in an absorbing subject,
to have friends,
to enjoy company,
to travel,
to be fully alive.
There are so many things
that I tell myself
I would really like to do,
but I can see the years slipping away
whilst I do nothing more adventurous
than talk about life,
rather than live it.
Lord,
the gift of life is precious.
Let me not waste
the years I have been given.

Lord of time,
I do not hope
to change the world.
But every day
I have the chance
to change my world.
I know that it is never too late
to start again.
Give me the energy
to tackle new ideas,
the courage to make mistakes,
the strength to climb out
of my comfortable rut,
to contribute to the world about me,
to come to life.

Lord,
I know that if I put myself
at your disposal,
if I say,
'Lord, guide me, use me',
then my life will change.
But I find it difficult
to offer myself wholeheartedly.
At the back of my mind
I have so many reservations.
If I say,
'Lord, take everything I have',
I do not really mean *everything*.
If I say,
'Let me do what you want',
I really mean, 'providing it's not too demanding.'

Lord,
in spite of my reservations,
in spite of my nervous commitment,
in spite of my weakness,
in spite of myself,
hear my prayer,
and bring me to life.

TIMES REMEMBERED

In everyone's life
there are times that are remembered
above others;
moments of excitement and delight;
recollections of the beauty of a place,
or a face,
or a time of immeasurable peace.
And always,
times remembered
are times shared.
For such elation, such lifting of the spirit
can only scale the peaks of joy
in the company of others,
or in the awareness
of the presence of God.

I can remember
learning to swim, and shouting,
'Look, look, I can do it!'
And smarting eyes and swallowed water
could not reduce that moment of triumph.
I can remember singing songs
on Christmas Eve,
in a room full of uncles, aunts and cousins
and wishing it would never end.
I can remember the incredible joy
of two people discovering
that their love was mutual.
I have shared dawn breaking over the sea
with a solitary bird,
and with the King of Creation,
in times remembered.

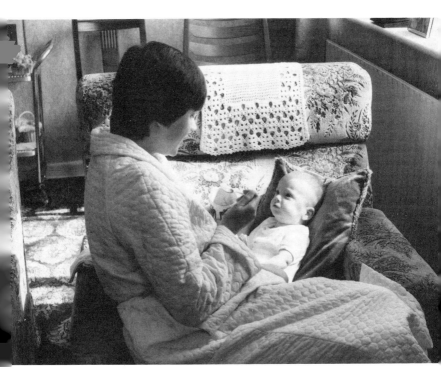

Lord,
you have been present
in every moment of happiness.
The laughter of a child
is your laughter.
The bond that unites
families, friends and lovers
is forged by you.
Times remembered
are times when
the eternal love which surrounds us
is experienced
for a brief moment.
Lord, the giver of joy,
may there be, this day,
at least *one* brief moment
to add
to my times remembered.

TIME FOR QUESTIONS

There are times
when everything seems pointless.
I find myself asking,
'Why am I alive?
Where am I going?
What am I doing with my life?
What is the point of my existence?
Am I merely existing,
Simply passing the time
between waking and sleeping?
Is there something I have to do,
to achieve, to learn?'
Dear God,
Do not let me live to be useless.

There must be more to life
than earning money,
eating food, buying clothes,
watching television.
In my head, over and over,
I hear the words,
'Do not be anxious
about what you shall eat,
or what you shall drink,
or what you shall wear.
Your heavenly Father knows
you need these things.
Seek first the kingdom of God.'
Is that why I am alive,
to search for meaning,
for God?
I have searched,
but at this moment
I seem to have taken a wrong turning,
I am in a blind alley, lost.

Lord,
if this search leads from here to eternity
I do not ask to see that far,
Simply show me the next step.
If your kingdom starts here,
guide me along the path
that I might not merely pass the time,
but find purpose and meaning
today.

MORNING TIME

Some people are like larks,
and others owls.
I wish I was a lark,
greeting the day blithely,
with a spring in my step
and a song on my lips,
attacking life
with vigour and confidence.
Instead, I'm like a bear,
a grizzly bear,
with half-closed eyes,
shuffling and grunting and irritable.
Lord,
at the start of this new day,
refresh me.

Refresh me Lord,
prevent me from growling
at people struggling
into their new day.
I have so much to be grateful for.
If, in the first hours of morning
I cannot sparkle,
help me, at least, to smile.
If I cannot make conversation,
help me, at least, to listen,
quietly and with patience.

Lord,
you know what it is
to spend sleepless nights –
you spent them on mountains
and in the wilderness.
You faced weariness,
suffering and crucifixion,
and met each of them
with love, or healing or forgiveness.
Lord,
this morning
refresh me with your spirit
that I might know
your forbearance,
your patience,
and your peace.

TIME FOR LAUGHTER

Thank God for laughter.
How dull the day that passes
without a smile;
how long the hours
without a spark of humour.
How subtle of God
to create beings
who could laugh at themselves,
even when things go wrong.
And if we are made
in the image of God,
is he a laughing God?
When God is not weeping
does he laugh at the antics of man?

Blessed are the laughter-makers
for they bring heaven to earth.
Blessed are those who greet us with a smile.
Blessed are those whose laughter
lives in our memories.
Blessed are those
whose chuckles and laughing eyes
tug the corners of our mouths.
Blessed are those who see
the funny side of things
for they redeem mistakes and failure.
Blessed are those who make us smile
for they reveal the face of love.
Blessed are those who make us laugh
for they reveal the joy of heaven.

Lord, help me
not to take myself too seriously.
If I am being pompous
prick that balloon
with laughter.
If I am being intense
about little things,
remind me, with a nudge,
how ridiculous I am.
When I am alone
let me see the sky and smile,
let me see trees and flowers
and laugh for sheer joy.
Let me know
that to be alone with God
is to be in the presence
of a father
who comforts us with love
and heals us, with a smile.

TIME TO BE

Somehow, over the years
I've become conditioned
to fill every minute
of my working day
with activity.
I've convinced myself
that doing nothing
is a waste of time.
But ceaseless activity
eats away my life,
gulps down whole days
so greedily
that weeks, and even months,
disappear,
with nothing to show
except the vague memory
that I was very busy.
Lord of time,
help me to make
time to be.

Every week,
I fill my diary
with people to meet
and things to do.
I keep on the move,
I make little lists
of tasks that must be done.
I wonder if
I'm afraid of being still?
I wonder if
I keep myself busy
to avoid the real questions?
I wonder if
my activities are an unconscious attempt
to prevent any kind of real thought?
Am I afraid
of simply being me
without an excuse?

Lord,
slow down my aimless race.
In my hurry,
my vision is blurred.
Slow me down, Lord.
Enlarge my life with stillness.
In serenity, help me to take stock,
to enjoy what is close at hand,
to delight in lingering
in the company of those I love,
to appreciate and to enjoy
every precious moment.
Lord of time, slow me down.

TIME TO PRETEND

I heard a story once
of a man who was so ugly
that he wore a mask,
a handsome mask.
In time he fell in love.
He was afraid to remove his mask,
but when he did
he was amazed to find
that his lover found his face
as beautiful as the mask.
He had become
like the mask he wore.
I wish I could wear a mask
that would make me more loving than I am.

Yet I do wear masks
and I do become
the mask I wear.
If I have to be friendly
when I'm not feeling friendly,
a few minutes in my friendly mask
and I become – like my mask.
If I need to be patient,
even when I'm irritable
if I wear my patient mask
in a short time
I become like the mask I wear.
In other words,
if I behave in a kindly manner,
providing my mask does not slip,
then I stand a chance
of becoming kind.

Suppose I dared to wear the mask of Christ.
Could I bear it?
Could I, like him,
die to myself?
Would I,
through the eyes
of the mask of Christ,
see the needs of people
and behind that mask
be moved to compassion,
to generosity, to forgiveness?

Lord,
you have offered me the mask of Christ,
but I am afraid;
give me the courage to wear it
that I might die to myself
and live in him.

TIME FOR MYSTERY

Lord of time,
we are surrounded by mystery,
from the vastness of galaxies
measured in millions of years,
to the flight of a migratory bird.
There is mystery
in the laws of the universe –
in laws that have existed
before man –
in laws that are defied
at our peril –
laws of space, of earth, of sea,
of life itself.
But without mystery,
what quality of life would we have?

Lord of time,
teach me not to be afraid of mystery.
Don't let my thoughts
be confined by reason,
by black and white lines of logic.
Let me rather
explore the rainbow gift
of imagination.
Children are perhaps
nearer to the Kingdom of God
because a child's hours and minutes
are splashed with awe and wonder,
and mystery is their delight.

Lord,
if man is the highest form of life,
then the universe shrinks
to the size of the human mind.
So thank God for mystery.
There is hope in mystery;
there is a promise of the future
in the mystery of the Infinite.
Lord,
in my press-buttoned,
computerised,
time-table dominated world,
let there be
time for awe and wonder.

TIME FOR CARING

The world news
is so often disheartening,
that perhaps
we could be forgiven
for avoiding it,
and for saying
'I can't see
what I can do about it.'
But if I close my mind
when papers print
news from far away,
will I turn my back
on things nearer home?
I can't avoid
the society in which I live,
nor detach myself
from the world.
But what can I do
that could affect the world?

What is the news?
It's what people are saying and doing
to each other,
for each other,
against each other,
with each other.
No matter how much I want to,
I can't shut my ears
or close my eyes
to the human race;
I can't bury my head in the sand,
like the ostrich.
But does any action I take,
anything I say or do
contribute to the world?
It must do:
no man is an island.

Lord,
when Mother Teresa
gave her first cup of water,
it was not world news.
When Francis of Assisi
embraced a leper,
he didn't make headlines.
When, from the cross,
you forgave the sins of mankind,
the world shrugged its shoulders,
and yet the world was changed forever.
Lord, help me to see
that every act of kindness,
every word of forgiveness,
every gesture of love,
seen or unseen,
is good news –
world news.

TIME FOR A CHILD

For Julia
a single day
embraces all the adventure,
laughter, pain and tragedy
of a life-time.
With nine birthdays
notched on her Brownie belt,
each new day is a world
to be explored, suffered
and conquered.
In games with her friends
her chatter
is bright and incessant,
stilled only by crouched contemplation
of a primeval snail
labouring from stone to stone
in a meadow pond.

For Julia
heart-rending tears
flow with inconsolable grief
for a broken toy,
a lost doll,
or a tiff with a bosom friend.
For Julia
justice and injustice
are sharply defined
with a clarity beyond the fathoming
of time-blunted grown-ups.
Her simplicity and directness,
her freshness,
her unconscious closeness
to her creator
convicts me
as worldly-wise and weary.
Yet in her innocence
is so much hope,
for the world
and for me.

'Unless you become
as little children,
you shall in no wise
enter the Kingdom of Heaven.'
Lord,
grant me patience
to learn from little children;
to feel again
the wonder of discovery;
to share the magnified minutes
of make-believe;
to know the joy
that brings hand-clapping,
shouts of delight;
to see your gaze
in the eyes of a child;
to hear your voice
in the love and truth of a child.

AGEING TIME

We grow old differently
on the inside
than we do on the outside.
On the outside
there are signs of wear:
the hair is thinner,
the face is lined,
the limbs won't do
what they used to do.
The flesh may be frailer,
but the inside of me,
the real me,
is not weakened by age
but strengthened.

I am not old, but older,
and the older, inner *me*
takes disappointment
in a stride.
Traumas,
that twenty years ago
would have stopped me in my tracks,
hardly slow me down
today.
Emotions that shook my frame
are harnessed, tempered
by bitter-sweet experience.
Paradoxically,
the ageing, inner me
can now recapture
something of the carefree nature
that came before the passions of youth,
in childhood and innocence.

Dear God, Holy Spirit,
the things of the spirit
are the only realities
that age cannot weary.
And the spirit that
reaches out to Spirit
is, in time, set free
from the flush and quiver
of ambition,
the fleeting joys of status and possessions,
and the physical indignities of age.
Lord,
as I grow older,
may I be blessed
with faith enough
to make the journey
from ageing body
to ageless life.

TIME FOR RENEWAL

Sometimes I wish
I could wipe the slate clean
and start again,
start a new life,
have a new personality.
It's only a fleeting thought,
because there are
so many things that I treasure
and wouldn't like to part with.
No, I don't want to wipe
everything from the slate –
just the bad days:
the sadness, the anger,
all the mistakes.

It would be good
to blot out every failure,
every hasty and wrong decision,
every row,
every pain I ever caused;
to reassemble, to recreate my life,
with all the good and acceptable facets
of my character.
And yet, without the faults,
without the flaws, without the pain,
would life be so rich,
or love so deep?

I know that I can't go back
and change one day of my life.
Yet I have only to ask,
and in your eyes
my sins and failures are removed,
not merely forgiven, but erased
as if they had never happened.
Even though I stumble
and offend against goodness
every day of my life,
your love does not weary.
So, Lord,
once again help me
with the love that cancels
every fault,
help me
to re-fashion my life
in your image.

TIME TO SEE CHRIST

If I say the name
Jesus Christ,
what images
leap into my mind:
hundreds of pictures,
northern Christs,
serene, fair-haired and blue-eyed
Italian Christs,
dark and curly
oriental Christs,
African Christs,
bearded,
sometimes clean-shaven –
I see him breaking bread
with his disciples,
agonizing in the Garden of Gethsemane;
or perhaps, I see a crucifix
too cruel to contemplate.

The image of Christ
can't be captured on canvas,
nor can sculptor's skill
confine him to wood and stone.
For Christ wears the face
of a hungry child.
He looks through
the bars of prisons.
He is with the dying
and the newly born.
He is in refugee camps
and in ordinary homes.
He is glimpsed in compassion,
in healing,
in every act of selfless giving.
He is love – resurrected.

Risen Lord,
let me live my life
aware of your triumph over death;
let me see you
whenever I see need,
that I might respond as I ought.
Let me see you in my work,
that I might witness to your presence.
Let me see you in my home
that I might speak and act
as a child of God.
Let me know you in my heart,
that the thoughts of my mind
might reflect your love.

TIME TO BE HONEST

How difficult it is
to say, 'I was wrong',
to make a straight-forward confession.
Even at the suggestion of fault
my every instinct
leaps to rationalize
every action, every word:
my deeds are misunderstood,
my words misinterpreted.
I'll say, 'I had no option;
I had to do that.'
I'll prevaricate:
'If she hadn't said that,
then I wouldn't have replied
as I did.'
It's hard to say, 'I was wrong,
Forgive me.'

What complex arguments,
what involved explanations
we launch into,
rather than admitting
we are at fault.
How defensive I am
if any statement of mine
is questioned.
How aggressive I become
if blame looks like
stopping at my doorstep.
Perhaps it's the instinct for survival,
or perhaps it's simply pride
that makes me believe my own excuses,
that convinces me that I'm always right.

Lord,
help me to face the truth about myself.
Help me to hear my words
as others hear them,
to see my face
as others see me;
let me be honest enough to recognize
my impatience and conceit;
let me recognize
my anger and selfishness;
give me sufficient humility
to accept my own weaknesses
for what they are.
Give me the grace –
at least in your presence –
to say, 'I was wrong – forgive me.'

TIME TO BE STILL

Holidays should be
refreshing, restoring, renewing.
Holidays should *recreate* us;
that's what recreation means.
Yet so often they exhaust us.
We come back in need of a rest,
making jokes
about needing a holiday
to get over the holiday.
But sadly, it's not really a joke.
We really are unrested.
Is it because we do not know
how to relax,
how to be calm,
how to be still?

We seek out
quiet and beautiful places;
but quietness around us
does not mean quietness within.
Even in silence
our minds are chattering,
arguing, planning.
'Be still, and know that I am God.'
If only we could
be still in our minds
if only we could, truly,
'rest in the Lord.'

Lord,
teach me how to still
my racing thoughts.
Help me to come to you
arguing nothing,
pleading nothing,
asking nothing,
except to be still
in your presence.
Give me the faith
that will enable me
to lay my burdens at your feet,
and to leave them there
in exchange for the peace
which passes all understanding.

TIME FOR PRAYER

Lord,
I often wish
I had more time to pray;
more time to collect my thoughts;
to evaluate my life.
But somehow, hours and days
slip through my fingers.
I am blessed
with home, food and friendship,
yet I take them for granted.
I wish I could take time
to appreciate, to remember,
to give thanks – to pray.

I wish I could intensify my life,
rather than letting the days
disappear in a blur
of unremembered incidents.
I wish I could take time
to see beauty and rejoice;
to hear laughter and give thanks;
to see people and pray.
I wish that even if I do not *say* prayers,
I could at least
look and listen prayerfully.

Lord,
help me to be alive
to your presence.
Help me to see you
in the faces of those about me.
Help me to hear you in the wind,
in the ripple of a stream
and in the voices of friend and stranger.
Help me to come alive.
Give me the courage
to stand in the path
of the wind of God
that I might pray with my life
and my life may become
a prayer.

TIME TO MAKE PEACE

Lord of time,
I want to make my peace with a friend.
But it's hard to bite back the arguments
that have crossed and re-crossed my mind,
to choke the cutting remarks
I've rehearsed in my head.
Life is too short
to waste precious hours
in ill-humoured conflict.
Lord,
help me to be truthful
in looking at my own failures;
help me to be generous-hearted
and to make my peace.

Lord,
forgive me for letting petty disagreements
grow into full-blooded rows.
Forgive me for being so full of myself
that I can't resist retaliating;
forgive me for the pride
that hardens my mouth,
for my meanness of spirit,
and the words I've spoken
that have caused pain or distress.
Forgive me for expecting apology
instead of saying, 'Sorry.'

Lord,
help me to make my peace with you.
Every expression of anger
is a denial of your love.
Every unlovely thought
is part of your Passion.
Every sin against my fellow
is part of your crucifixion.
Lord,
even from the cross
you forgave, and offered Paradise.
Help me to recognize
the love you offer,
and to share it
as generously as it is given.
Help me to make my peace,
and to live in love.

TIME FOR OTHERS

Lord of time,
I'm quite good at saying,
'Something ought to be done about it'
but not so good
at taking the initiative
and doing something myself.
I hear myself saying,
'She's lonely.
She needs to get out and about
and meet people',
yet I do not invite her
to my home.
I can't afford the time.
When I say,
'She should meet people',
I really mean, *other people*,
not me.

Lord,
forgive me
for my half-hearted concern.
Forgive me
for being so miserly
with my time,
for being impatient
in conversation with the elderly.
Forgive me
for groaning inwardly
when I see someone who is troubled
approaching me.
Forgive me
for not listening wholeheartedly,
for mentally looking at my watch,
inwardly tapping my foot
and backing away.
Forgive me
for the hypocrisy
of pretending concern
whilst making sure
I will not get involved.

Lord,
you have always taken the initiative.
You did not delegate others
to visit the sick,
or to comfort the sorrowful.
You came into our lives,
you healed
by listening, talking, touching.
You could not resist
the crisis of the lonely and the troubled;
you gave not only time,
but your last breath.
Lord,
help me to respond to need generously.
As you have time for me,
may I have time for others.

HARVEST TIME

At this time of year
churches and chapels
are so filled with the fruits of harvest
that ministers must tread carefully
across overflowing sanctuaries.
Communion rails and altar steps
are festooned
with flowers, hops and ferns.
Choir stalls rise
above hills and pyramids
of apples, pears and tomatoes.
Cucumbers are positioned
with green-fingered pride
beside bread shaped as sheaves of corn,
for it is time to be thankful.

As farmers look at the fruit of fields
and gauge its worth,
so I must consider my harvest –
the harvest of days and years –
the harvest of time.
Taken in all,
it has been good.
There have been doubts and fears,
mistakes, and pain,
but they have withered
overcome by deep-rooted trust,
overshadowed by the blossom
of laughter
and friendship.
Like the farmers, I've been known to complain,
yet, through all the disappointments,
the harvest of the years
has been rich in experience and love.

Lord,
your harvest
is the harvest of love;
love sown in the hearts of people;
love that spreads out
like the branches of a great tree
covering all who seek its shelter;
love that inspires and recreates;
love that is planted
in the weak and the weary,
the sick and the dying.
The harvest of your love
is the life that reaches
through the weeds of sin and death
to the sunlight of resurrection.
Lord,
nurture my days with your love,
water my soul with the dew of forgiveness,
that the harvest of my life
might be your joy.

THE TREASURES OF TIME

Another day's post
stares up at me from the breakfast table.
Without opening them
I can see from their cellophane windows
that they are about Insurance, Assurance,
Renewals and Bank Statements.
There is one, thank God, hand-written,
from one of my sons.
And suddenly it is very clear
what things matter most.
Insurance companies may go bust,
money is worthless
in itself,
status a shallow fraud
but love is without price.

The older I get,
the more I'm inclined to be obsessed
with security and safety,
taking precautions
against poverty in old age.
But this morning's post
makes it very clear
that the greatest investment
I can ever make
is love:
in the love of my wife and children,
in the love of friends,
in the love of God.
For love bears all things,
hopes all things, endures all things;
Love never ends.

In itself,
money is worthless.
Without laughter and familiar faces
time is meaningless.
Without faith, and hope and dreams
the future is poverty-stricken.
Lord,
may I never seek
the security of things
at the expense of those I love.
Teach me instead
to store up days that never fade,
shared minutes
that moth and rust cannot corrupt.
Bills and bank balances
may come and go,
but the treasures of time
are measured in love.

TIME TO FORGIVE

How terrible are the words,
'I'll never forgive him.'
Withholding forgiveness
reduces people,
scars the face with bitterness,
cripples the mind,
gives root to a bitter canker
that grows within,
hell-bent on self-destruction.
How terrible the words,
'I'll never forgive him.'

The time to forgive is now,
immediately, unconditionally;
for unforgiving memory
rekindles anger that deafens and blinds;
unforgiving memory
relights the fires
of pains past.
Only forgiveness
can open the flood-gates
of pent-up hurt and irritation.
Released, their force is spent
in the deep, broad surge of forgiveness.
The time to forgive is now.

Lord,
your forgiveness is always immediate:
'Go, your sins are forgiven you.'
'Rise up, your sins are forgiven you.'
'Father, forgive them.'
'*This* day, you will be in paradise with me.'
You do not forgive seven times,
or even seventy times seven;
your forgiveness is never ending.
As I turn to you,
knowing that I will receive your forgiveness,
wipe clean not only my sins
but erase forever from my lips
the words,
'I'll never forgive him.'

TIME FOR FRIENDS

When I was young,
I used to think
I had lots of friends.
Time sorts them out;
time's seeing eye
examines them, tests them
and measures them.
Through distance, work, adventure and experience
time reduces the number,
drawing a line through some names
and underlining others.
The final count is very small.

With some friends
ten years separation is as yesterday;
time cannot dim the flame.
With others a year, or even a day,
is all time needs
to extinguish friendship forever.
Time tests most severely
when things go wrong.
When there are accidents and failures,
when marriages fall apart,
when jobs are lost,
when loved ones die,
time reveals who is true and who is not.
Only a few friends stood at the cross,
only a few stood firm
in spite of everything.

Lord,
when I have failed friends
I have failed you.
Give me the courage to be a true friend.
In those times when friends are needed,
let me not be afraid of opinion, nor of failure.
Let me not run from sorrow or grief,
but let me stand, with you,
beside my friends
in their hour of need.
Let my friendship be a pledge
of my faith in you.

A TIME OF FEAR

Fear is such an unaccountable thing.
I don't mean fear of pain,
or loss, or future things.
I mean the fear that sweeps down
and covers me like the black shadow
of some great albatross
hovering unexpectedly
and without reason.
And all I want to do is close my eyes
and hope that everything
will go away.

But that solves nothing.
Fear is irrational.
It feeds on doubt and darkness,
hides behind the eyes.
So I must face my fear
and come to terms with it.
The moment I find courage
to think and reason,
fear recedes.
If I can smile at myself
fear retreats even further.
If I can do one unselfish act of love,
then fear is defeated.

Lord,
in the Garden of Gethsemane
you shared with everyone
who has ever been afraid.
You conquered fear with love
and returned saying,
'Do not be afraid.'
In the light of your love
death has lost its sting
and so has fear.
Lord,
May your love
be the key that releases me
from fear.

TIME ALONE

Surrounded by those I love,
it seems ungrateful
to want to be alone.
It is not merely a selfish desire,
there is a need to be alone;
to be away from the comings and goings
of family and friends;
to be free from the never-ending voice
of city and town:
to escape the incessant clamour
of newspapers, radio and television.
I am not cynical or tired of life,
I simply need to hear my own conscience,
to reassess, to find myself.

I am tempted
to escape from thought
by being so busy and involved
that vital questions
are pushed into a dust-covered mental recess
marked pending.
Crisis and sorrow,
triumph and success
need to be prepared for,
need to be considered before the event.
It is foolhardy
to push away ultimate questions
about my own life and existence
until the flame of my years
begins to stutter.
It is self-evident
that the deeper the question,
the greater is the need
to be alone.

Standing on a hill
overlooking a city
I see bricks and concrete
surrounded by fields
like a small cluster of stones
on a green baize table;
and the big city is not so big.
Sitting in the timeless silence
of an ancient chapel
I hear the still small voice
that has been drowned in the roar of humanity.
And returning, I find
I am no longer alone.

TIME FOR JOY

So much of my time
is spent not seeing,
not hearing, not enjoying.
I can drive through sweeping hills
and lush green fields,
and hardly notice them.
Deaf to the sound
of breeze and bird song,
some fretful thought shuts out
a world of beauty
and a chance of joy is lost.
Lord of time,
in whose presence a minute
can be measureless,
let me not waste my life
on small concerns.

So much of my time
is spent in needless hurry;
in saying, 'Excuse me;
can't stop, sorry,
–so much to do; must rush.'
The joy of casual conversation
is cut short,
because somehow
I think *chatting* is merely
wasting time.
My efficiency robs me of pleasure.
Lord, teach me
that time spent talking
of books, or sport,
of last night's television,
is not time lost,
but time enriched.

In my self-conceived sense of hurry,
my self-important bustle,
there is no time to talk,
no time to listen, or to look,
no time to enjoy;
no time to be aware of the peace of God
in places, people,
or within myself.
Lord of time,
help me to rest in your presence,
to find time to share,
time to smile,
time for prayer,
time for joy.

TIME FOR GOD

Dear God,
so many of my decisions are impulsive;
so many of my judgements are ill-informed;
so much of my understanding lacks wisdom.
When I have decisions to make,
help me to decide calmly.
When I am about to make a judgement,
let me see what is good and positive.
When I interpret the words
and actions of my friends,
may I be as generous to them
as you are to me.

Dear Lord,
my eyes deceive me,
my ears mislead me,
my tongue lets me down,
my thoughts are confused –
unless you are with me,
unless you direct
my looking, speaking, hearing,
all I think
and say and am.
Lord, I ask you to possess,
to enter that fraction of time,
that millionth part of a second
before I think or speak,
so that the knowledge of your presence
may influence all I do.